Addition & Subtraction FLASHCARD GAMES

by Susan Dillon

New York • Toronto • London • Auckland • Sydney
Mexico City • New Delhi • Hong Kong • Buenos Aires

Teaching *Resources*

I'd like to dedicate this book...
to Jackson, Liam, and Luke for their inspiring love of learning;
to Mike for his support and enthusiasm;
and to my "Math for Laughs" kids for playing (and laughing).

Cover design by James Sarfati
Interior design by Solutions by Design, Inc.
Interior illustration by Alicia Dorn

ISBN: 0-439-64015-6

2 3 4 5 6 7 8 9 10   40   11 10 09 08 07 06 05 04

Contents

Introduction

Learn the facts in a flash...with flashcard games! Simple to learn and to teach, and enriching for all math levels, these 25 games put a new spin on facts practice and require little preparation or equipment. Plus, these games are written so children can learn and play on their own! Photocopy and distribute the game pages for fun practice in class or at home.

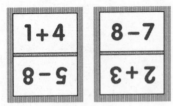

Two flashcards in one!

ABOUT THE GAMES

The banner at the top of the page tells you that the game or games on the page are suitable for *pairs*, *small groups* (four to eight players), or *large groups* (nine or more).

All games include

- ⊕ *Object of the game:* A brief explanation of the game and its purpose.

- ⊕ *You'll need:* The specific flashcards called for, plus other equipment or preparation requirements.

- ⊕ *Instructions:* Easy-to-follow directions written for children in grades 2 to 3 (younger players may need some initial adult guidance).

- ⊕ *Variation:* An easy way to change the game for variety and/or to increase or decrease the level of challenge.

- ⊕ *Fair Play Tip:* Simple advice on how to keep a more competitive or high-energy game in check.

- ⊕ *Flashcard Hint:* How to put together certain games with specific flashcard requirements, using the flashcard collection on pages 25–48.

Skills practice: Every game can be played with addition or subtraction flashcards—or both mixed together! While most games focus strictly on facts practice, you can work in a review of inequalities and place value respectively by playing *Jump or Duck* and *Place Card* (page 21). You can also combine math and language arts in one lesson with *ABC Flash* and *Story Addition* (page 22).

A note to teachers, parents, or supervising adults: These games have been created for unsupervised play, which means that older children will be able to read the instructions and play these games with minimum guidance. (Younger children may need reading help and initial supervision.) You can tailor the games to the specific needs of your group. For instance, some games specifically ask players to solve an equation in a specified amount of time. You can increase or decrease the given time to suit the level of the group or even that of individual children.

You can customize the flashcard set for a specific skill or level of difficulty by weeding out harder or easier problems, or adding more problems of your own (see page 6, *Create Your Own Flashcards*).

TIPS FOR PLAYING

Here are some great ways to help children get the most out of these flashcard games.

Choosing Who Goes First

If every player wants to be first, you may need to step in to help assign this coveted role. You might choose a specific child who is having a little trouble concentrating. (You might also look for games that require a game timer, another active role for children who need help focusing.) A simple way to select the player who goes first is to let each player choose one flashcard from a facedown set; the player with the highest answer goes first. See *Memory Flash* (page 7) and *Major Math Baseball* (page 20) for other creative suggestions.

You might also let children earn the position of first player. Create an "I Go First!" sticker (use any standard label) to be given daily or weekly to children as a reward for outstanding work or behavior. The sticker is the child's "ticket" to being the player who goes first when it's flashcard game time.

Checking Answers

In many cases, an incorrect answer results in a penalty. Players must be in charge of checking other players' answers, which is great practice and a way to keep all minds in the game at all times. You might want to make a copy of the *Facts Table Answer Key* on page 49 available in case there is a disagreement about the answers.

PLAYING-CARD GAMES—WITH FLASHCARDS

You'll find a number of fun and familiar games for pairs and small groups. These games, adapted from traditional playing-card games, include old favorites such as *Go Fish* (see *Go Fish a Flashcard*, page 15).

Here are a few tips on playing-card basics to model for young players.

⊕ **Shuffle** the flashcards in various ways. The most thorough method is to put half the set in each hand (thumbs on top), bend the flashcards slightly inward with your index finger knuckle, and fold in the two sets together. Demonstrate this and let players try it out. Show them other methods you know. If this proves too difficult for small hands, spread out flashcards facedown on a desk and mix them around.

⊕ **Deal** the flashcards the first time, showing players how to pass facedown flashcards to each player, one at a time. Let children take turns practicing this role, with your guidance. Make sure to identify "faceup" (problem-side up) and "facedown" (problem-side down), since these are important key words in the directions. In games for pairs in this book, the dealer always goes first. In playing-card games with more than two players, the player to the dealer's right goes first.

⊕ **Fan** a hand of flashcards to get ready to play. Have each player spread out the cards so the problems are visible to him or her only. Players hold their flashcards at the bottom corners by the thumb in front and support the cards with flat fingers in back. (Make sure children use the hand that's most comfortable.) Remind players to hold flashcards straight up and close enough to the face so others can't peek; you may need to remind them frequently in the first game or two.

Small hands having trouble holding the cards? Check out Einstein Design's Card Holda, a crafty device that holds up to 20 cards and offers a small, easy-to-grip handle for child-size hands.

Punch-Out Flashcards

The special set of ready-to-go flashcards on pages 25–48 can be used to play all of the games in this book—or simply to practice facts.

Special features include

⊕ 2-in-1 flashcards: an addition and a subtraction problem appear on the same flashcard, with one problem right-side up and the other upside down. Addition problems are purple and subtraction problems are black, so they are easy to identify. Want to mix up the practice? Simply turn some flashcards addition-side up and others subtraction-side up.

⊕ no answers: Many games in this book are "hands-on," meaning players pick up flashcards; thus, answers can't be visible. Note that page 49 contains answers for all addition and subtraction facts from 0 through 12; those problems included in the flashcard set are highlighted.

⊕ playing-card-size flashcards: smaller dimensions make the flashcards easy to hold.

Create Your Own Flashcards

Need more problems than we provide? Want additional sets of flashcards for multiple games? Photocopy the flashcard template on page 6 onto card stock and write in your own equations. Be sure to laminate these homemade flashcards so they withstand the wear and tear of movement-based games such as *Hopcards* (page 19) where the flashcards are literally underfoot and "grabby" games like *Tag Plus* (page 16). For easy laminating, try self-adhesive laminating sheets, which can be found at any office-supply store.

Use a Standard Set of Flashcards

Any standard set of flashcards will work fine with these games. With games where children are holding their own flashcards, hide answers with sticky notes cut to fit the shape of the card. Make a similar adjustment to cover the backside of a two-sided card if there is another equation showing.

Let the games begin!

CREATE YOUR OWN FLASHCARDS

Need another set of flashcards or some additional problems? Use this template!

1. Print out copies on card stock.
2. Write in your own problems.
3. Cut out each flashcard.

4. Laminate for durability.
5. For a key to addition and subtraction facts with answers 0–12, see page 49.

Memory Flash

OBJECT OF THE GAME: In this flashcard version of the popular game *Concentration*, players collect pairs with the same answers to win.

YOU'LL NEED: 16 flashcards—eight same-answer pairs (e.g., 4 + 3 and 6 + 1)

INSTRUCTIONS:

1 The player who goes first shuffles the flashcards and places them facedown into a grid—four rows vertical, four rows horizontal.

2 The first player flips over one flashcard in the grid and calculates the answer, then flips over another flashcard and calculates the answer, saying it out loud. The object is to match two flashcards with the same answer.

3 If the player gets a match (and answers correctly), he or she takes the flashcards and goes again. If the player doesn't get a match or gives an incorrect answer, he or she flips the flashcards back over and the second player gets a turn.

4 The game continues as players take turns to find all the matches. The game is over when all flashcards are gone from the grid; the player with the most matches wins.

VARIATION

If players need more challenge, try *Extreme Memory Flash*—use 24 cards (12 same-answer pairs). Each player gets a five-second time limit for calculations, timed by the other player.

All flashcards on pages 25–48 include at least one same-answer pair except 0 in addition and 12 in subtraction.

Who goes first?
Suggestion: Play *Guess the Equation*

1. A game leader thinks of a single-digit addition or subtraction equation such as 4 – 3 = 1.

2. Players take turns guessing the equation. Players must be sure to supply the full equation, including the answer.

3. The leader may provide hints such as "higher," "lower," and "one number right" to steer players closer to the equation.

4. The first player to guess the equation goes first.

For playing-card basics, choosing who goes first, checking answers, and more, see pages 4–5.

Pair Down

OBJECT OF THE GAME: Players race to pair up all of their same-answer flashcards.

YOU'LL NEED: two sets of 16 flashcards, each containing eight same-answer pairs

INSTRUCTIONS:

1. Each player shuffles a set of 16 flashcards containing eight same-answer pairs. The players divide their decks in half, setting up the first eight flashcards faceup into two horizontal rows in front of them. Then they place the remaining eight flashcards faceup over the first set, so there are eight piles of two faceup flashcards in front of each player.

2. At the signal (count together "1-2-3 GO!"), both players start gathering pairs of flashcards with the same answers from their own faceup card piles. When a pair is made, it reveals two more flashcards underneath, which can now be paired with the other cards. Players keep their pairs in a nearby pile.

3. The first player to make pairs with all his or her flashcards wins. If there is a calculating error (check pairs after the game), the other player wins. If a player gets stuck with no pairs showing, he or she loses. If both players get stuck, no one wins and they start over.

VARIATION

For advanced players, try a competitive game of *Pair Down*. Shuffle the 32 flashcards (16 same-answer pairs) all together and then split the deck so that each player gets 16 cards. Players set up the flashcards as described above. On the count of three, players gather pairs from both boards. The player with the most pairs when the boards are clear (or when no more pairs are showing) wins.

Tic-Tac-Facts

OBJECT OF THE GAME: Players solve problems to earn turns at tic-tac-toe.

YOU'LL NEED: 10 or more addition and subtraction flashcards in separate piles, pencil and paper

INSTRUCTIONS:

1. The first player draws a traditional tic-tac-toe board. The first player is "+" for this game; the other player is "−" (instead of X and O).

2. The first player shuffles the addition flashcards and places them facedown by his or her side; he or she shuffles the subtraction flashcards and places them facedown beside the other player.

3. Players earn turns putting a "+" or "−" symbol in any one of the nine squares. The aim is to get three in a row across, up and down, or diagonally. To earn a turn, each player must first correctly answer the top flashcard equation in the addition or subtraction pile by his or her side. If the player gets an incorrect answer, he or she misses his or her turn.

4. The player who gets three in a row wins. Now the other player is "+" and goes first; he or she shuffles and switches the piles, and starts another game.

VARIATION

To speed up the calculations, play *Tick-Tock-Facts*—each player gets 5 seconds (as timed by the other player) to answer the problem.

For playing-card basics, choosing who goes first, checking answers, and more, see pages 4–5.

Addition & Subtraction Flashcard Games   Scholastic Teaching Resources

Slap You Five

OBJECT OF THE GAME: Players race to be the first to slap the flashcards that equal 5, and win the pile.

YOU'LL NEED: set of 36 flashcards, including five or more flashcards with the answer 5

INSTRUCTIONS:

1 Two players sit facing one another. One player is the dealer. The dealer shuffles the flashcards and divides them into two even facedown piles, one for him- or herself and one for the other player. The players hold their pile of cards facedown in their hands.

2 Starting with the dealer, the players take turns discarding their top flashcard into a faceup pile between them.

3 With each discarded flashcard, both players race to calculate the answer in their heads. The object is to "slap" (quickly place a hand over) the flashcard if the answer is 5. The first to slap the flashcard gets the pile; that player puts the pile at the bottom of his or her handful of flashcards and takes the next turn.

4 If a player slaps the pile with another flashcard answer besides 5, the other player gets the pile.

5 The player with the most flashcards at the end of a designated time period wins.

1 + 2	The following
4 − 3	flashcards in this book

have the answer 5:
0 + 5, 1 + 4, 2 + 3, 3 + 2,
5 + 0, 12 − 7, 11 − 6, 10 − 5,
9 − 4, 8 − 3, 7 − 2, 6 − 1.

FAIR PLAY TIP
Players must keep their hands on the table at their sides while calculating the answers.

VARIATION

Add money skills practice to this game by playing "Slap You Fives." Along with flashcards, distribute play money (which can be bought in any party goods store) so that each player gets a facedown pile of about fifteen $10 and $20 bills, and at least five $5 bills. To discard, alternate between flashcards and bills; with each bill, call out the total dollar amount. Five-dollar bills get the slap. As in the game rules above, the fastest slap keeps the pile, and a wrong slap awards the pile to the other player.

For playing-card basics, choosing who goes first, checking answers, and more, see pages 4–5.

Silly Signals

OBJECT OF THE GAME: Players do silly moves corresponding with specific answers, which earn them flashcards.

YOU'LL NEED: set of 72 flashcards (more or less), including at least five cards each with the answers 5, 6, and 7 (or see Variation); silly signals for answers (see step 3)

INSTRUCTIONS:

1 Two players sit facing each other. One player is the dealer. The dealer shuffles the flashcards and divides them into two even facedown piles, one for the other player and one for him- or herself. The players hold their flashcards facedown in their hands.

2 Starting with the dealer, the players take turns discarding one flashcard from their pile, forming a faceup pile between them.

3 With each discarded flashcard, players must quickly calculate the answer in their heads. If the answer is 5, 6, or 7, the players race to do the corresponding silly signal.

Here are some silly signal ideas for the answers 5, 6, and 7:

    5: stand up, turn around, sit down

    6: pat head and rub belly

    7: drum lap then snap fingers

4 The first player to complete the signal gets the pile. If a player miscalculates and starts to do a signal, or the wrong signal is done, the other player gets the pile.

5 When players discard flashcards with answers other than 5, 6, or 7, they do not signal and the pile is left untouched.

6 The player with the most flashcards at the end of a designated time period wins.

> $1+2$
> $4-3$
>
> Among the flashcards on pages 25–48, there are at least five addition flashcards with answers 5 through 12 and subtraction flashcards with answers 0 through 7.

VARIATION

This game works with any answers. Select any three answers with which players could use extra practice, and use those numbers in place of 5, 6, and 7. Players can make up their own silly signals for these answers.

For playing-card basics, choosing who goes first, checking answers, and more, see pages 4–5.

Addition & Subtraction Flashcard Games   Scholastic Teaching Resources

Hangermath

OBJECT OF THE GAME: Each player gets 10 chances to guess the other player's answer—before a complete hanging coat is drawn!

YOU'LL NEED: set of 72 flashcards (more or less), including at least one problem for each answer 0 through 12; pencil and two sheets of paper

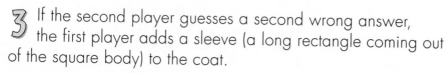

Among the flashcards on pages 25–48, there is at least 1 flashcard for every answer.

INSTRUCTIONS:

1 One player goes first. He or she draws a coat hanger (a triangle with a hook on the top) on one piece of paper and writes down any answer from 0 through 12 on the underside of the other piece of paper, making sure the other player can't see.

2 The second player holds the flashcard set and tries to guess the answer. For each guess, he or she looks through the flashcard set and picks out a flashcard that equals that answer. For instance, if the player wants to guess the answer 11, he or she might say, "Is it 7 + 4?" and show that flashcard. If the player is wrong, the first player hangs a sleeveless coat (a big square) off a hanging hook.

3 If the second player guesses a second wrong answer, the first player adds a sleeve (a long rectangle coming out of the square body) to the coat.

4 With every wrong answer, the first player adds other pieces to the coat: another sleeve, a collar, two pockets, and four buttons, or any 10 items the player chooses. (Hint: The player who is guessing may place the "guessed" flashcards faceup in front of him or her to avoid guessing an answer twice.)

5 If the second player guesses 10 times incorrectly, then he or she loses and the first player picks a new number for another game. If the second player guesses correctly before the tenth guess, he or she wins and the players switch roles.

VARIATION

To speed along the game for younger children, use 13 flashcards only—one of each with the answers 0 through 12.

Add That Garbage!

OBJECT OF THE GAME: Players hunt for the answer 7 among the flashcards in a basket.

YOU'LL NEED: set of 36 addition flashcards (more or less), including only one with the answer 7; paper recycling bin or any box or basket

INSTRUCTIONS:

1 Dump the flashcards in one basket and mix well.

2 Without peeking inside the basket, the first player picks out one addition flashcard at a time, answers the problem, then throws it aside. The object is to find the flashcard with the answer 7.

3 If the first player picks seven cards without getting the answer 7, the second player takes a turn.

4 The first player to find the flashcard with the answer 7 wins.

VARIATION

Choose other answers to hunt for and assign each answer a certain number of points (e.g., 10 points for the answer 10). Players switch after earning any points or making a calculating error. The player with the most points when the basket is empty wins.

Take-Away Toss

OBJECT OF THE GAME: Players attempt to toss the greatest number of answered flashcards in their own basket.

YOU'LL NEED: set of 30 subtraction flashcards (more or less); two small baskets or boxes; clock or timer

INSTRUCTIONS:

1 Two players stand facing each other about six feet apart. In front of each of player is a basket in which the opposing player attempts to toss flashcards to score points.

2 One player is the first card-tosser; the other is the referee. The card-tosser holds all the flashcards facedown.

4 On the signal, the tosser turns over his or her first flashcard and solves the subtraction problem.

5 If the answer is correct, the referee puts two arms straight up, allowing the player to turn and toss the flashcard into his or her basket. If the flashcard goes in, he or she gets a point.

6 If the player's answer is incorrect or the flashcard misses the basket, the referee crosses his or her wrists at chest-level. The players switch roles.

7 The game ends when all flashcards have been pitched at the baskets. Whoever gets the most points (flashcards in the basket) wins.

VARIATION

Players can also play *Add Toss* using addition flashcards and following the rules above.

For playing-card basics, choosing who goes first, checking answers, and more, see pages 4-5.

Addition & Subtraction Flashcard Games   Scholastic Teaching Resources

Flashcard Football

OBJECT OF THE GAME: Similar to the favorite lunchtime game, players slide flashcards across a table after solving the problems—if the edge sticks over, they get points.

YOU'LL NEED: set of 72 flashcards (more or less); a table or desk with a slick surface, or a shiny floor (see Variation)

INSTRUCTIONS:

1 The first player shuffles and divides the flashcards facedown between him- or herself and the other player. Players stand on opposite sides of the table.

2 The first player turns over a flashcard and gives the answer. If the player answers correctly, he or she earns a chance to score, and slides the flashcard across the table. If any part of the flashcard sticks out over (but does not fall off) the edge, that player gets a touchdown and earns 6 points. If it doesn't reach the end of the table, or if it falls off, it's the second player's turn.

3 When players score a touchdown, they may try for the extra point: The opposing player forms goalposts by pointing his or her index fingers toward one another with thumbs facing up and palms facing in; the "kicking" player attempts to "flick" the flashcard through the goalposts from 5 inches away. (Flicking is done by holding the flashcard upright with the left hand, then hitting it with the snapping motion of the right index finger off the thumb, or vice versa for lefties.) That player goes again.

4 At any time, either player can challenge the other player on his or her answer. If the player indeed answered incorrectly, the other player gets to "kick" a field goal (following the extra point directions in step 3) and gets the next turn. A field goal earns 3 points.

5 Players continue taking turns sliding their flashcards. If either player's flashcards run out, he or she can use discarded flashcards that have been shuffled.

6 The player with the most points at the end of a designated time period wins.

VARIATION

If there is no ideal table surface for the game, use the floor. (Test it to see if the flashcards slide well.) Make "table edges" by sticking a long piece of masking tape on two opposite sides of the floor (not too far apart); flashcards that touch the masking tape earn points.

For playing-card basics, choosing who goes first, checking answers, and more, see pages 4–5.

Uno y Uno

OBJECT OF THE GAME: In *Uno y Uno* (pronounced *OO-noh EE OO-noh*—Spanish for "1 + 1") each player gets rid of flashcards by matching answers from his or her hand with answers or first numbers in the discard pile. The winner is the player who gets rid of all his or her flashcards first, or whose last flashcard(s) contain the number 1.

YOU'LL NEED: set of 72 flashcards (more or less)—including the flashcard 1 + 1 and at least eight other flashcards with 1 + another number (e.g., 1 + 5, 9 + 1, and so on)

INSTRUCTIONS:

1 Players sit in a circle facing each other. One player is the dealer. He or she shuffles and deals seven flashcards per player facedown, then puts the rest of the set facedown in the middle to form a draw pile. (Players should fan their cards in their hands so others can't see.) The dealer turns over the top card and places it next to the draw pile to form a discard pile.

2 The player to the right of the dealer goes first. The first player must discard one flashcard with the same answer or the same first addend as the top flashcard in the discard pile. For example, if the top discard flashcard is 3 + 4, the player can discard any flashcard from his or her hand with the answer 7 (the sum) or 3 (the first number). The player must announce the answer to the equation.

3 If the player doesn't have a card to discard, he or she must take one card from the draw pile.

4 The game continues going around the circle clockwise until one player has no more cards. That player wins. A player can also win two other ways: with the flashcard 1 + 1 remaining in his or her hand or with two or more flashcards that show 1 plus any other number—for example, 1 + 8 and 11 + 1. The player announces "¡Uno y Uno!" and shows his or her flashcard or flashcards to win.

1 + 2
4 – 3

The flashcard *Uno y Uno* (1 + 1) can be found on page 25. At least eight other addition "uno" flashcards (1 + 2 through 1 + 11) can be found on pages 25–48.

VARIATION

Try this game with subtraction equations (*Uno Menos Uno*) or higher numbers such as 9 (*Nueve y Nueve*). Make sure you have enough "___ – 1" or "9 + ___" flashcards in your set for the new game.

For playing-card basics, choosing who goes first, checking answers, and more, see pages 4–5.

Addition & Subtraction Flashcard Games   Scholastic Teaching Resources

Sum Pig

OBJECT OF THE GAME: Players try not to be the last to put their thumb to their nose when one player gets four sums of a kind.

YOU'LL NEED: one set of four same-answer addition flashcards per player (e.g., 16 flashcards for a four-player game, with four flashcards equaling 7, four equaling 9, and so on)

INSTRUCTIONS:

1. Players sit in a circle facing each other. One player is the dealer. The dealer shuffles and deals four flashcards per player facedown. (Hint: Players should fan their cards in their hands so others can't see.)

2. Each player sorts flashcards by grouping those that match (have the same sums), and preparing to discard a flashcard that doesn't match. The goal is to make a hand of four flashcards with the same sum.

3. At the same time, all players discard to the left one unwanted flashcard facedown. Then they pick up the flashcard that is placed at their right.

4. Each player adds the new flashcard to his or her hand, looks for a match, and prepares to discard another flashcard, still working toward getting four of a kind. The game goes on as players discard unneeded cards and pick up their neighbors' discarded cards.

5. The first player to get four of a kind quietly puts a thumb to his or her nose. As soon as that happens, the rest of the players race to put their thumbs to their noses.

6. The last player to put up his or her thumb loses that round and earns an "S." The first player to lose six times, thus spelling S-U-M P-I-G, loses.

Go Fish a Flashcard

OBJECT OF THE GAME: Players ask other players for flashcards with the same answers to get pairs.

YOU'LL NEED: set of 72 flashcards (more or less)—to make pairs, each flashcard answer should match at least one other flashcard answer in the set; scrap paper for keeping score

INSTRUCTIONS:

1. Players sit in a circle facing each other. One player is the first dealer. The dealer shuffles and deals seven flashcards per player facedown, putting the rest of the set facedown in the center of the players to form a draw pile. Players should fan their cards in their hands so others can't see.

2. Players check their hands for pairs with the same answers. Players place their collected pairs in their own pair pile.

3. The player to the right of the dealer goes first. The first player asks any other player for a flashcard with the same answer as one of the cards in his or her hand. For example, a player with the card 2 + 2 might ask another player, "Do you have a card that equals four?" If the second player has the card 1 + 3, he or she must hand it over. The first player puts the cards in his or her pair pile and goes again. If the second player does not have the card, he or she says, "Go fish a flashcard," and the first player must draw a card from the pile and make a pair, if possible.

4. Players take turns going around the circle clockwise until one player gets rid of all of his or her flashcards. Players then count their pairs. Players earn 5 points per pair and lose 1 point for every flashcard remaining in their hands; the player with the best score wins the game and is the dealer for the next game. Keep track of players' scores on a tally sheet to determine an overall winner.

For playing-card basics, choosing who goes first, checking answers, and more, see pages 4–5.

Tag Plus

OBJECT OF THE GAME: Players race the clock to collect same-answer flashcards from other players by tagging their feet.

YOU'LL NEED: 22 flashcards—11 pairs of same-answer cards; clock or timer

INSTRUCTIONS:

1 Players sit cross-legged in a circle facing each other. Make the circle small enough so that each player can lean forward and reach every other player's feet.

2 One player goes first. (In the spirit of the game, you might want to give this honor to the player with the biggest shoe size!) The player next to him or her clockwise in the circle keeps time and may sit just outside the circle.

3 The first player gives each player two flashcards, then holds the rest facedown in a pile.

4 The other players hold up their two flashcards, one in each hand, so the first player can read them. The timer gives the signal and then the first player turns over his or her first flashcard. The first player must quickly calculate the flashcard problem, say the answer out loud, and then look for a match (a flashcard held up by another player with the same answer).

5 To get a matching flashcard, the first player must tag the foot of the player holding the flashcard. The player collects each pair earned in a nearby pile. If there are no same answers among the other players' flashcards, the player puts the flashcard faceup nearby.

6 The first player turns over the next flashcard and continues to tag feet to make pairs. If the matching flashcard is faceup, the player must tag one of his or her own feet to make the pair.

| 1 + 2 |
| 4 − 3 |

If you're using the flashcards on pages 25–48, select 11 pairs of flashcards with answers 1 through 11 (addition or subtraction) for this game.

7 The turn ends when the player has made 11 pairs. The timer records the time.

8 The player who was timing now takes a turn, shuffling the flashcards, dealing them out, and starting another game; the player next to him or her clockwise in the circle keeps the time.

9 Every player gets a turn. The player with the fastest (lowest) time wins.

FAIR PLAY TIP
This is a timed game that requires cooperation from all the players. Any player who doesn't give over his or her flashcards easily to another player may have five seconds added to his or her time.

For playing-card basics, choosing who goes first, checking answers, and more, see pages 4–5.

Addition & Subtraction Flashcard Games   Scholastic Teaching Resources

Pluses and Minuses

OBJECT OF THE GAME: Players go box by box through the homemade gameboard by solving equations. A box with pluses lets you climb to a higher box; a box with minuses brings you to a lower box. Get to the 50th box to win.

YOU'LL NEED: set of at least 30 flashcards; large sheet of construction paper and marker to make gameboard; selection of small, flat objects such as buttons for playing pieces

MAKE THE GAMEBOARD:

1 Draw a large vertical rectangle on construction paper; divide into a grid of 5 boxes (horizontal) by 10 boxes (vertical) for 50 spaces. Put the numbers 1 through 50 in the boxes, starting with the bottom left corner and ending with the top left corner (at the end of a row, number the box right above it and proceed in the opposite direction on that row). Add a home spot before the first box. This is where players will start.

2 Draw in three sets of plus signs (+), climbing from one space to any higher space—for instance, climbing from box 2 to box 12. Draw three sets of minus signs (–) that slide from a higher box to a lower box—for instance, box 28 down to box 15. (See sample gameboard at right.)

PLUSES and MINUSES	50	49	48	47	46
	41	42	43	44	45
	40	39	38	37	36
	31	32	33	34	35
	30	29	28	27	26
	21	22	23	24	25
	20	19	18	17	16
	11	12	13	14	15
	10	9	8	7	6
Home	1	2	3	4	5

INSTRUCTIONS:

1 Players place a set of facedown flashcards at the side of the board, and set their playing pieces at the home spot.

2 The first player turns over a flashcard and answers the problem. The answer is the number of spaces to move the playing piece on the board. For instance, with the flashcard 9 + 3, the player would move 12 spaces.

3 Players take turns answering flashcards and moving along the board from box 1 through 50, climbing the pluses or sliding down the minuses when they land on a box that marks the beginning of an ascent (+) or a descent (–). For instance, if the player lands on box 2, he or she can automatically go to box 12, but not if the player lands on box 9.

4 The winner is the first to get to the 50th box.

VARIATION

Make a life-size gameboard on a large roll of paper. Players are their own playing pieces (each box must be large enough for one or more players to stand in). Players can feel free to "climb" (an invisible ladder) on the pluses to the higher box, and "slide" (don't tear the paper!) to the lower box on the minuses.

For playing-card basics, choosing who goes first, checking answers, and more, see pages 4–5.

Mathematical Chairs

OBJECT OF THE GAME: Players race to sit in the chairs when the music stops . . . but in this version of the famous game, players must solve equations correctly to earn their chairs.

YOU'LL NEED: set of 72 flashcards (more or less); two back-to-back rows of chairs (one chair less than the number of players); clock or timer

INSTRUCTIONS:

1 One player is the leader. The leader holds a set of flashcards. He or she is also in charge of starting and stopping the music (humming is fine). As the music plays, the rest of the players walk around the chairs. When the leader stops the music, each player scrambles to sit in a chair. The leader hands a facedown flashcard to each sitting player.

2 The player who doesn't have a chair stands to the side. However, in this game, he or she is not out yet!

3 One at a time, the players must turn over their flashcards and solve the problem within five seconds. If any player answers incorrectly, the player who didn't get a chair gets a chance to solve the answer in five more seconds to earn that chair. If he or she solves the problem correctly, the two players switch.

4 The new standing player waits for a chance to earn a seat if another player misses his or her equation. The last player standing when all the flashcards have been answered is out.

5 The leader removes a chair; the game resumes until there is a winner. The winner is the next leader.

VARIATION

Try *Mathematical Chairs* with no chairs! Put the flashcards (one less than the number of players) facedown in two rows about 2 feet apart. The players walk around the flashcards. When the music stops, players scramble to be the first to put a foot on the flashcard. The rest is the same (steps 3–5). For fun, try this version without shoes!

FAIR PLAY TIP
A player who gets pushy vying for an empty chair can be called out of the game by the leader.

For playing-card basics, choosing who goes first, checking answers, and more, see pages 4–5.

Number One Goose

OBJECT OF THE GAME: In this version of *Duck, Duck, Goose*, the "duck" finds the "goose" by solving equations held by the players in the circle.

YOU'LL NEED: set of 72 flashcards (more or less)—one flashcard per child per game (note: in each game, one of the cards must have an equation that equals 1).

 The set of flashcards in the back of the book contains two addition (1 + 0, 0 + 1) and many subtraction flashcards with the answer 1.

INSTRUCTIONS:

1 One player is the first duck. All the players except the duck sit facing each other in a circle. Each player gets one flashcard and keeps it facedown in his or her lap (no peeking). The duck stands outside the circle.

2 The duck goes around the circle tapping each player on the shoulder and saying, "duck," as in the traditional game. The duck stops at one chosen player and says, "Are you the Number One Goose?" That player turns over his or her flashcard and asks the duck the problem.

3 The duck must answer the problem. If the flashcard equals a number besides 1, the sitting player must chase the duck around the circle of students. If the player tags the duck, he or she is the new duck. If the duck isn't tagged, he or she remains the duck and the player sits back in his or her space and sets aside the flashcard—that player can't be called on in the next round.

4 When the duck finds a player with the flashcard equation that equals 1, he or she has found the "Number One Goose" and wins. To play again, collect and shuffle the cards. The players each get a new flashcard, and the current goose is the duck in the next game.

For playing-card basics, choosing who goes first, checking answers, and more, see pages 4-5.

Hopcards

OBJECT OF THE GAME: Players solve equations while hopping on a hopscotch grid.

YOU'LL NEED: set of 72 flashcards (more or less)—10 flashcards per turn

MAKE YOUR OWN HOPCARDS GRID:

Place flashcards faceup in a traditional hopscotch pattern, spacing them evenly (leave about two feet between the flashcards). For flashcards with only one problem per card, place two flashcards in each space—one facing the front of the grid and the other facing the back. Secure the flashcards with masking tape if necessary.

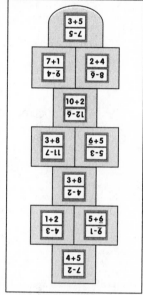

INSTRUCTIONS:

1 Players form a line behind the first square of the grid.

2 The first player hops on one foot, landing right in front of the first flashcard, then looks down and answers the equation. Then the player jumps with both feet up to the next two problems, answers both, hops to the next flashcard and answers the problem, and so on to the last problem. After solving the final problem, the player jumps with both feet to the end, and then turns around in one jump.

3 To complete the turn, the player answers the second round of problems as he or she hops back.

4 If at any time the player answers an equation incorrectly, he or she starts again at the beginning.

5 When the first player finishes, the next player sets up a new *Hopcards* board and gets a turn. Shuffle flashcards between turns.

Major Math Baseball

OBJECT OF THE GAME: Players get to round the bases by answering the problems first.

YOU'LL NEED: set of 72 flashcards (more or less)

INSTRUCTIONS:

1 Clear a space in the room so there is room to fit a small imaginary baseball diamond—about 5 feet to each imaginary base.

2 Three players are the first pitcher, catcher, and batter respectively; the rest of the players line up to be a batter behind home plate.

3 The pitcher stands in the center of the diamond holding the flashcards facedown. The catcher stands behind home plate. The first batter goes up to home plate, ready for the first pitch. (The batter can feel free to hold an imaginary bat.)

4 The pitcher pitches—reading the first problem from the flashcard set to the catcher and batter. The catcher and batter race to answer the equation first. If the batter answers first, and correctly, he or she gets a home run. The batter runs around the bases, and then goes to the end of the line of batters. The on-deck batter (the next batter in line) gets up to the plate.

5 If the catcher answers first and correctly, the batter is out and goes to the end of the batting line; the catcher steps up as the next batter, and the on-deck batter becomes the catcher.

6 If at any time the batter or catcher answers incorrectly, the pitcher switches with that player and hands over the flashcards. That player is now the pitcher.

7 The player to get the most home runs in nine innings (nine times through the batting order) wins.

Who goes first?
Suggestion: Play *Fast Ball*

1. Make several sets of flashcards from page 6 on cheap copy or printer paper and fill them in with your own addition or subtraction problems. Cut out the flashcards (five per player, with some extras) and crumple each into a ball. Set the balls in a basket and place them beside the pitcher.

2. One at a time, the players come up to the plate. Have an umpire start timing. A pitcher throws five "fast balls" one at a time right to the batter.

3. The player must catch each ball (or grab it from the ground if he or she misses), open up the paper, and answer the problem. The umpire stops timing when the last equation has been answered correctly.

4. The player with the lowest (fastest) time for answering all five problems wins. The order of winners decides the first pitcher, catcher, batter, and the order of the batting lineup.

FAIR PLAY TIP
Assign an umpire (perhaps the last batter in line) to determine the first player to say the answer, or to make the call if an answer is incorrect.

For playing-card basics, choosing who goes first, checking answers, and more, see pages 4–5.

Addition & Subtraction Flashcard Games   Scholastic Teaching Resources

Jump or Duck

OBJECT OF THE GAME: Players solve two problems. They jump if the second is greater than the first, and duck if it's less.

YOU'LL NEED: set of 72 flashcards (more or less)

INSTRUCTIONS:

1 Players stand in a line, side by side. One player is the leader. The leader stands facing the line of players, holding the deck of flashcards.

2 The leader shows all the players a flashcard, and gives players ample time to calculate the answer in their heads. The leader then puts the flashcard aside, facedown.

3 The leader shows another flashcard for a few seconds, again giving players time to calculate the answer. The leader puts the second card aside, announcing, "Jump or duck!" Players must determine if the second flashcard's answer is greater than or less than the one before. Players jump if they think that the second answer is greater than the first, and duck (bend down holding their knees) if it's less than the first.

4 The leader asks players who ducked or jumped incorrectly to sit down.

5 The game continues, getting faster and faster as players are eliminated. The last player standing is the winner, and becomes leader for the next game.

FAIR PLAY TIP
To avoid players "copycatting" others and to make the game more challenging, after each round ask one random player for his or her answers in a greater-than or less-than statement. The player will need to say, for instance, "8 is greater than 3." If the player cannot answer or if his or her answer is incorrect, the player is out.

For playing-card basics, choosing who goes first, checking answers, and more, see pages 4–5.

Place Card

OBJECT OF THE GAME: Players race to solve the flashcard problem and determine its place value in a five-digit number.

YOU'LL NEED: set of 72 flashcards (more or less); chalkboard or erasable board

INSTRUCTIONS:

1 One player leads the first game. The leader writes any five-digit number on the board—for instance, 52,417. (There must be one "1" and no repeating numbers in the big number. The leader holds the set of flashcards.)

2 One at a time, the leader shows a flashcard to the class. If the answer is also a digit in the number on the board, players race to tell its place value (ones, tens, hundreds, thousands, ten thousands). For instance, if the number is 52,417, and the leader holds up the flashcard 4 + 3, the players who have figured out the answer (7) race to raise their hands and give the correct place value: ones. If the flashcard answer does not appear in the number, players race to answer "no place." If the answer is a two-digit number, such as 12, the correct answer is "tens and thousands."

3 Once all the place values have been identified, the leader writes another big number.

4 Each time a player is the first to answer correctly, he or she earns a "P," then "L," "A," "C," and so on until the player has spelled the name of the game, P-L-A-C-E C-A-R-D. If a player answers incorrectly, he or she loses a letter.

5 Mix up the set of flashcards periodically. The first player to spell "Place Card" wins, and gets to be leader for the next game.

FAIR PLAY TIP
If one or two players are dominating the game, create a rule by which a player who gets a letter can't be called on first for the next equation.

ABC Flash

OBJECT OF THE GAME: Players must solve problems and come up with words that start with certain letters of the alphabet...at the same time!

YOU'LL NEED: set of 72 flashcards (more or less)

INSTRUCTIONS:

1 Players sit in a line, side by side. One player is the first leader. The leader stands in front of the line of players, holding the set of flashcards facedown.

2 The leader turns over a flashcard so it is visible to all the players and says the chorus: "When you walked to school, what did you see?" The leader then points to a random player to answer.

3 The chosen player must use the answer along with an object that starts with the letter "A" in his or her response. So, for example, if the flashcard is 4 + 5, the player might answer, "Nine antelopes looking at me."

4 The leader repeats the chorus, pointing to another player. The next chosen player's response includes the answer to that flashcard and a word starting with the letter "B" (for example, "Fifteen bears looking at me"). Play continues, each time with a new flashcard and the next letter of the alphabet.

5 If any player answers the problem incorrectly, gives a word beginning with the wrong letter of the alphabet, or delays for more than 5 seconds, that player is out of the game. The last player in the game is the winner and becomes the leader in the next game.

Story Addition

OBJECT OF THE GAME: Players use flashcard answers to create a story.

YOU'LL NEED: set of 72 addition flashcards (more or less); blackboard or erasable board

INSTRUCTIONS:

1 Players sit at their seats. To start, one player stands in front of the others, holding the set of flashcards facedown.

2 The leader starts the story, with an opening (for example, "Once upon a time a class of very smart students were playing a game"). Then he or she hands all the flashcards to another player.

3 The player takes the top flashcard, calculates the answer, and then adds a sentence to the made-up story. The trick is that the player must use the answer in the sentence. For instance if the flashcard is 4 + 5, the player might add the following sentence to the story: "The students saw nine birds on the school rooftop." Then that player passes the set to another player who continues the story.

4 Players continue passing around the flashcards and telling the story until everyone gets a turn. For example, the story above might continue "Seven [1 + 6] students got up from their seats to see what the birds were doing," "Then three [2 + 1] of the birds flew over to the window sill," and so forth.

5 Play several times over the course of a day or weeks. One player can write down the story each time you play. Then let the group vote on their favorite story, and make copies for each player to keep.

For playing-card basics, choosing who goes first, checking answers, and more, see pages 4–5.

Addition & Subtraction Flashcard Games   Scholastic Teaching Resources

Calculating Obstacles

OBJECT OF THE GAME: Players compete in an obstacle course that includes problem solving.

YOU'LL NEED: set of 72 flashcards (more or less); obstacle course; clock or timer

INSTRUCTIONS:

1 Clear a long and wide space (approximately 50 x 75 feet). One player is the leader. The leader creates the two obstacle courses (see How to Make an Obstacle Course at right). The leader explains and demonstrates the task for each obstacle before the game begins. He or she may assign a player to record the times for each team.

2 Players count off to divide into two lines of even teams. Each team lines up in front of one of the obstacle courses. On the signal (the leader counts, "1-2-3 GO!"), the first player from each team goes up to the first obstacle in his or her course, picks up the top flashcard from the pile, and shows the other players. Then the player calls out the answer, puts the flashcard at the bottom of the pile, and repeats the obstacle task for the number of times indicated by the flashcard answer. The player does the same with all obstacles.

3 After finishing the course, each player runs back to his or her team and tags the next player in line who then goes though the course, turning over a new flashcard from each pile. If at any time one of the players does an obstacle incorrectly because of miscalculation, the leader or the other team can have him or her stop, recalculate, and repeat the obstacle again. If a player's teammates catch an error, they can stop him or her right away by raising their hands.

4 The first team whose members all complete the course wins. The fastest player on the winning team gets to be leader for the next game.

How to make an obstacle course:

1. For each game, a leader creates two identical obstacle courses in two straight lines. Each course will have four obstacles. A small pile of facedown flashcards is placed next to each obstacle. The object is for players to move through the obstacle course according to the answer to the flashcard that they pick up beside each obstacle.

2. The leader should make the obstacles fun but not too difficult, placing common objects at each station and assigning simple movements to do for each obstacle. (Players should be able to do the activity at each obstacle easily and in repetition.) For instance, the answer to a flashcard next to a jump rope might tell the player how many times to jump rope. Or, the flashcard next to a tennis ball and a box might tell the player how many times to toss the tennis ball into the box. The leader can ask other players for help with creating the course.

Flash-n-Dash

OBJECT OF THE GAME: Players "flash" flashcards, solve the problems, then "dash" the number of steps of the answers.

YOU'LL NEED: set of 72 flashcards (more or less); clock or timer; two desks or small tables; blackboard or erasable board

INSTRUCTIONS:

1 Clear a large space, approximately 15 feet long. Place two desks on opposite sides of the space. On each desk place half the set of flashcards in a facedown pile. Players line up in back of one of the desks. (Make sure there is plenty of room along the sides of the desks for players to walk quickly from one desk to the other.)

2 One player is the leader. The leader is in charge of timing each player and making sure the flashcards are answered correctly. When time begins, the first player in line dashes (walks quickly) up to the pile of flashcards at the opposite desk. The player picks up the top flashcard, reads it aloud, and calls out the answer. Then, keeping the flashcard in hand, the player turns around and goes to the other desk, picking up the top flashcard and solving the problem out loud in the same way, collecting it, and moving on as quickly as possible.

3 The player continues back and forth between the desks solving problems. When time ends in 1 minute, or if the player gets an incorrect answer, the player stops and records on the board his or her score—the number of flashcards in hand minus any incorrect answers. The player returns the collected flashcards to the leader, and goes to the end of the line. (The leader can set these cards aside or add them to the piles on the desks if the card supply gets low. Make sure to shuffle well.)

4 Every player gets a turn. The player with the highest score wins, and gets to be leader for the next game.

For playing-card basics, choosing who goes first, checking answers, and more, see pages 4–5.

Bumpers

OBJECT OF THE GAME: Players take steps determined by the flashcard answers to collect the flashcards from other players; the fastest time wins.

YOU'LL NEED: set of 72 flashcards (more or less); clock or timer

INSTRUCTIONS:

1 Clear a large space. The first player hands each other player one facedown flashcard and keeps one, setting the rest of the flashcards aside. When the first player gives the cue, "Scatter!" the rest of the players scatter around the space, finding a spot to stand anywhere in the area.

2 Another designated player is in charge of keeping time. When time begins, the first player, the "bumper," must read out loud the problem on the flashcard he or she is holding, call out the answer, and then take the number of steps determined by the answer—for instance, 9 steps if the flashcard is 4 + 5. The bumper may move anywhere around the space, aiming to gently bump another player on the final step. (The bumper may take bigger or smaller steps to get to the player, but must take the exact number of steps.) The player who is bumped hands over his or her flashcard and "falls" to the ground (sits down).

3 The bumper reads out loud that flashcard's problem, calculates the answer, and takes the required steps to bump into another player and take the flashcard; again, the bumped player falls.

4 Play continues until the bumper calculates the last problem (no steps required). The timer stops the clock and adds five seconds for every incorrect number of steps taken. He or she records the bumper's score—the total time—on the board.

5 Now the timer gets a turn as the bumper, and the last player bumped who hasn't had a turn as the timer keeps time. After every player gets a turn as the bumper, the player with the fastest (lowest) time wins.

Addition & Subtraction Flashcard Games   Scholastic Teaching Resources

PUNCH-OUT ADDITION/SUBTRACTION FLASHCARDS

Here's how to create your set of 72 flashcards:

1. Punch out each flashcard by gently tearing around the perforated edge until the card comes loose.

2. Laminate flashcards for durability.

3. To make extra flashcards, photocopy the flashcard template (page 6) on card stock and fill in the cards with needed equations. Cut out and laminate for durability.

4. For a key to addition and subtraction facts with answers 0–12, see page 49.

25

$$0 + 1$$

$$12 - 12$$

$$1 + 0$$

$$10 - 10$$

$$1 + 1$$

$$\overline{6} - \overline{6}$$

$$2 + 0$$

$$8 - 8$$

$$1 + 2$$

$$\overline{9} - \overline{9}$$

$$3 + 0$$

$$5 - 5$$

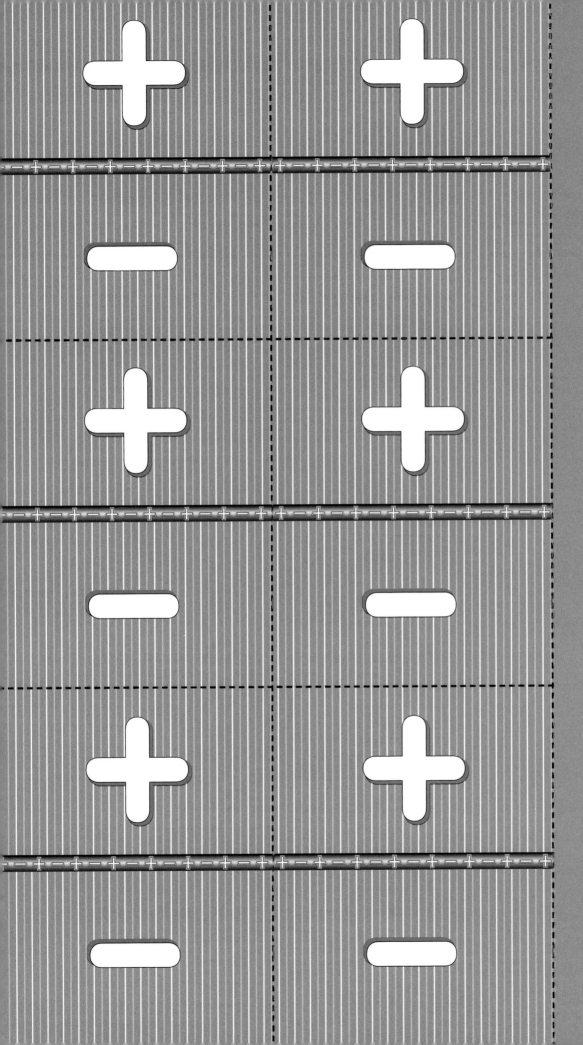

PUNCH-OUT ADDITION/SUBTRACTION FLASHCARDS

Here's how to create your set of 72 flashcards:

1. Punch out each flashcard by gently tearing around the perforated edge until the card comes loose.
2. Laminate flashcards for durability.
3. To make extra flashcards, photocopy the flashcard template (page 6) on card stock and fill in the cards with needed equations. Cut out and laminate for durability.
4. For a key to addition and subtraction facts with answers 0–12, see page 49.

$$1 + 3$$

$$3 - 3$$

$$2 + 2$$

$$1 - 1$$

$$3 + 1$$

$$11 - 10$$

$$0 + 5$$

$$10 - 9$$

$$1 + 4$$

$$9 - 8$$

$$2 + 3$$

$$8 - 7$$

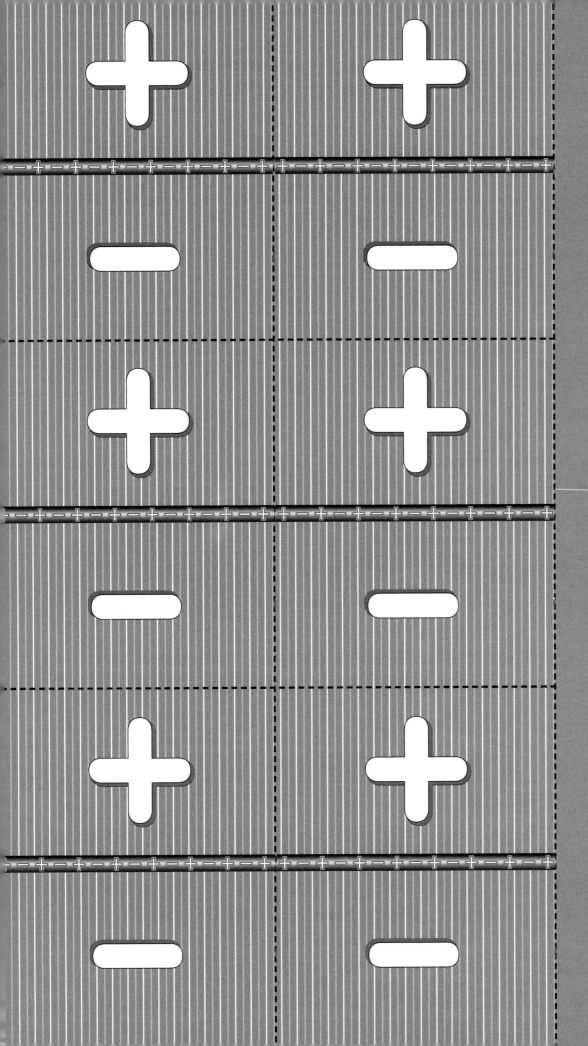

PUNCH-OUT ADDITION/SUBTRACTION FLASHCARDS

Here's how to create your set of 72 flashcards:

1. Punch out each flashcard by gently tearing around the perforated edge until the card comes loose.

2. Laminate flashcards for durability.

3. To make extra flashcards, photocopy the flashcard template (page 6) on card stock and fill in the cards with needed equations. Cut out and laminate for durability.

4. For a key to addition and subtraction facts with answers 0–12, see page 49.

29

| $3+2$ | $5+0$ |
| $7-6$ | $6-5$ |

| $1+5$ | $2+4$ |
| $5-4$ | $4-3$ |

| $3+3$ | $4+2$ |
| $3-2$ | $2-1$ |

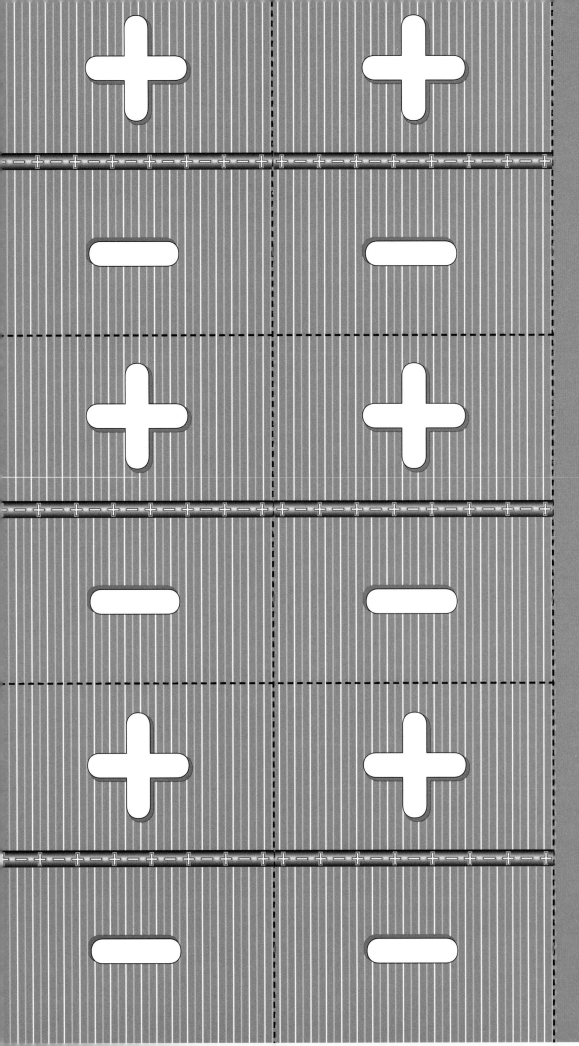

PUNCH-OUT ADDITION/SUBTRACTION FLASHCARDS

Here's how to create your set of 72 flashcards:

1. Punch out each flashcard by gently tearing around the perforated edge until the card comes loose.
2. Laminate flashcards for durability.
3. To make extra flashcards, photocopy the flashcard template (page 6) on card stock and fill in the cards with needed equations. Cut out and laminate for durability.
4. For a key to addition and subtraction facts with answers 0–12, see page 49.

31

$5 + 1$

$12 - 10$

$0 + 7$

$11 - \overline{9}$

$1 + \underline{6}$

$10 - 8$

$2 + 5$

$9 - \overline{7}$

$3 + 4$

$8 - \overline{6}$

$4 + 3$

$7 - 5$

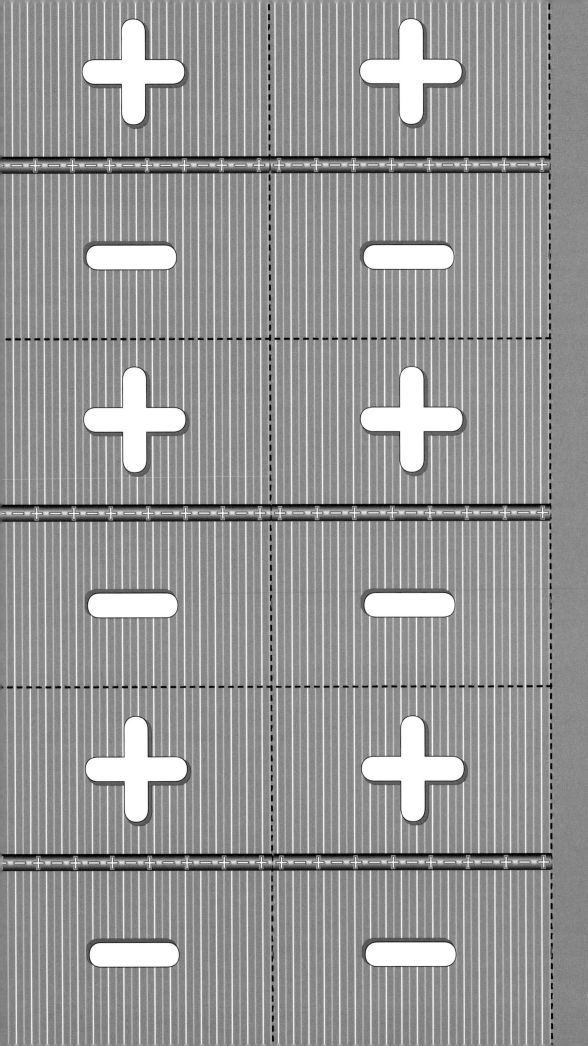

Addition & Subtraction Flashcard Games   Scholastic Teaching Resources

PUNCH-OUT ADDITION/SUBTRACTION FLASHCARDS

Here's how to create your set of 72 flashcards:

1. Punch out each flashcard by gently tearing around the perforated edge until the card comes loose.
2. Laminate flashcards for durability.
3. To make extra flashcards, photocopy the flashcard template (page 6) on card stock and fill in the cards with needed equations. Cut out and laminate for durability.
4. For a key to addition and subtraction facts with answers 0–12, see page 49.

5 + 2

6 − 4

6 + 1
9

5 − 3

1 + 7

4 − 2

2 + 6
6

12 − 9

3 + 5

11 − 8

4 + 4

10 − 7

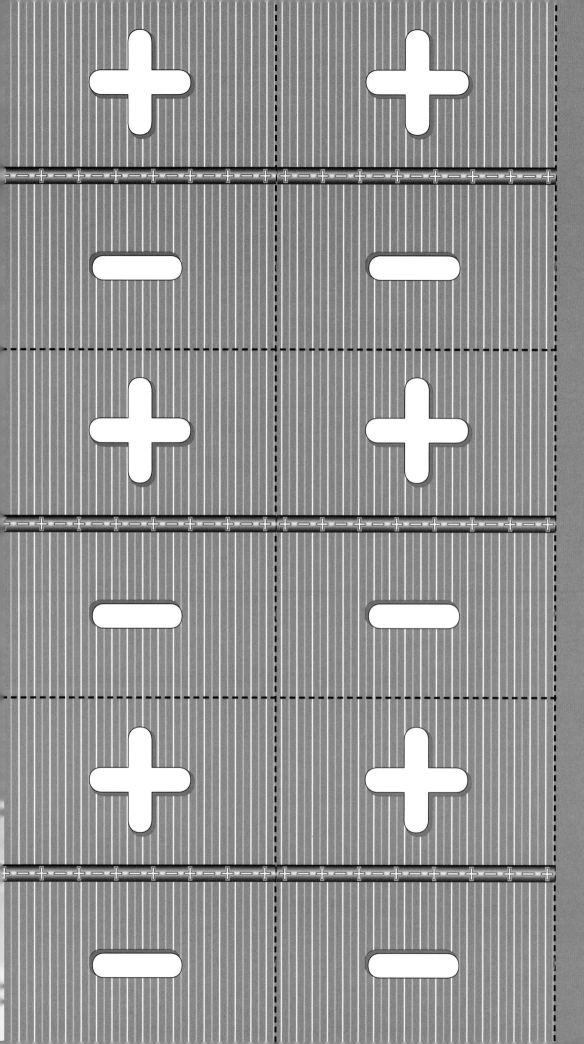

PUNCH-OUT ADDITION/SUBTRACTION FLASHCARDS

Here's how to create your set of 72 flashcards:

1. Punch out each flashcard by gently tearing around the perforated edge until the card comes loose.
2. Laminate flashcards for durability.
3. To make extra flashcards, photocopy the flashcard template (page 6) on card stock and fill in the cards with needed equations. Cut out and laminate for durability.
4. For a key to addition and subtraction facts with answers 0–12, see page 49.

35

$5 + 3$

$9 - 6$

$6 + 2$

$8 - 5$

$7 + 1$

$7 - 4$

$8 + 0$

$9 - 3$

$0 + 9$

$5 - 2$

$1 + 8$

$12 - 8$

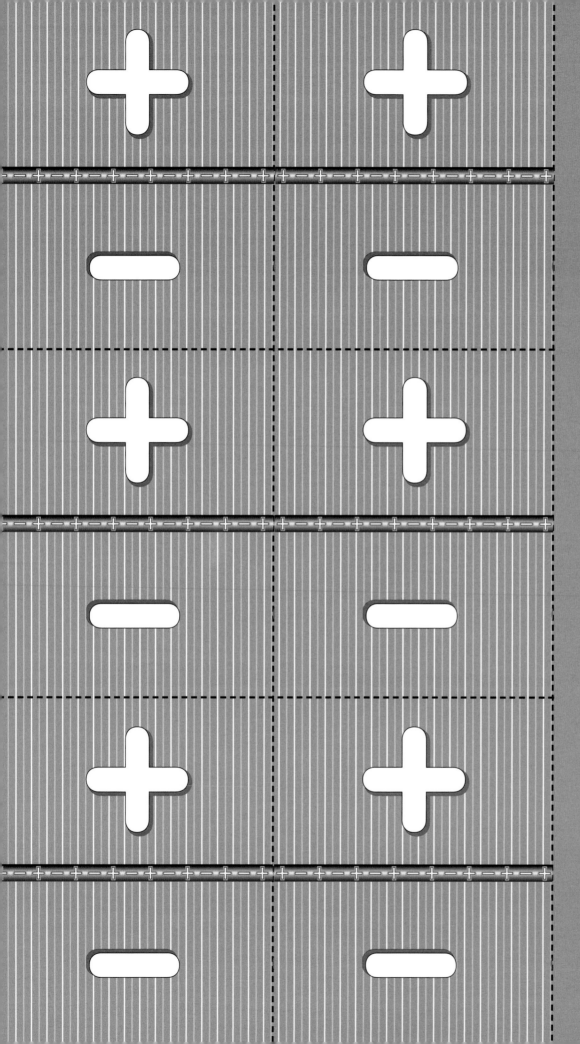

Addition & Subtraction Flashcard Games   Scholastic Teaching Resources

PUNCH-OUT ADDITION/SUBTRACTION FLASHCARDS

Here's how to create your set of 72 flashcards:

1. Punch out each flashcard by gently tearing around the perforated edge until the card comes loose.
2. Laminate flashcards for durability.
3. To make extra flashcards, photocopy the flashcard template (page 6) on card stock and fill in the cards with needed equations. Cut out and laminate for durability.
4. For a key to addition and subtraction facts with answers 0–12, see page 49.

$2 + 7$

$11 - 7$

$3 + \underline{6}$

$10 - \underline{6}$

$4 + 5$

$9 - 5$

$5 + 4$

$8 - 4$

$\underline{6} + 3$

$7 - 3$

$7 + 2$

$\underline{6} - 2$

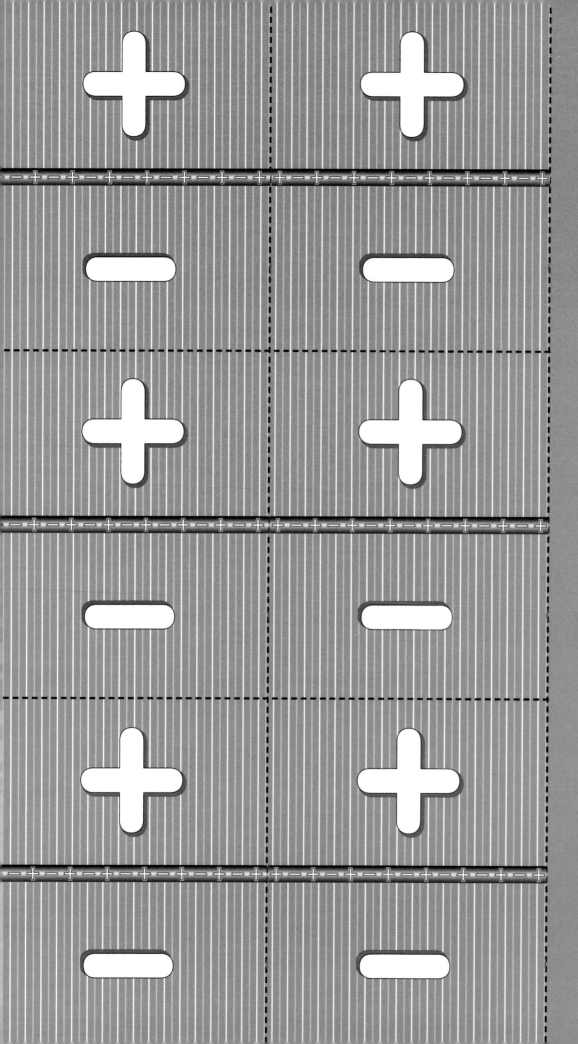

PUNCH-OUT ADDITION/SUBTRACTION FLASHCARDS

Here's how to create your set of 72 flashcards:

1. Punch out each flashcard by gently tearing around the perforated edge until the card comes loose.
2. Laminate flashcards for durability.
3. To make extra flashcards, photocopy the flashcard template (page 6) on card stock and fill in the cards with needed equations. Cut out and laminate for durability.
4. For a key to addition and subtraction facts with answers 0–12, see page 49.

39

$8 + 1$

$12 - 7$

$1 + \underline{9}$

$11 - \underline{6}$

$2 + 8$

$10 - 5$

$3 + 7$

$9 - \underline{4}$

$4 + \underline{6}$

$8 - 3$

$5 + 5$

$7 - 2$

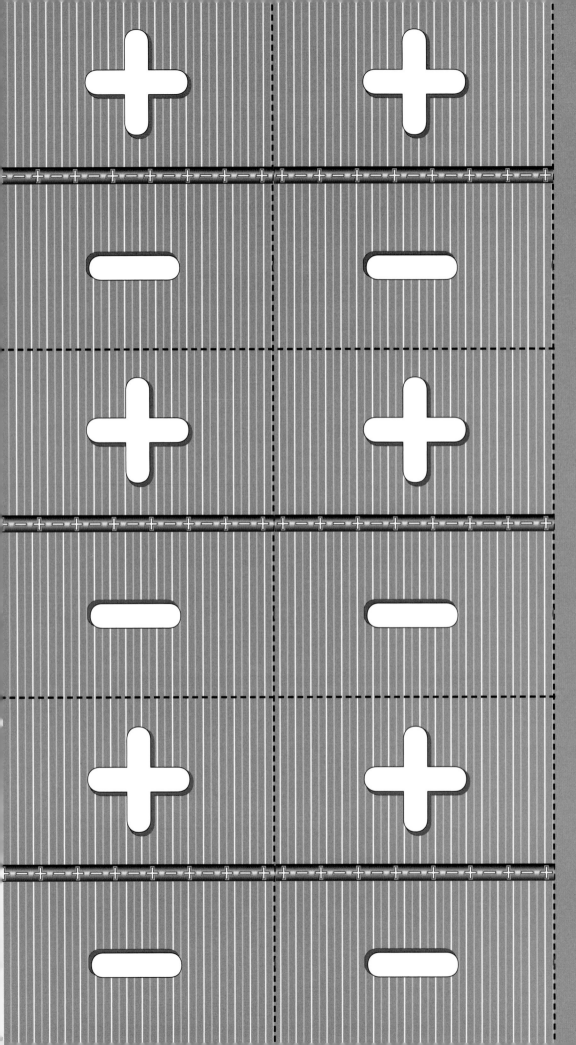

PUNCH-OUT ADDITION/SUBTRACTION FLASHCARDS

Here's how to create your set of 72 flashcards:

1. Punch out each flashcard by gently tearing around the perforated edge until the card comes loose.
2. Laminate flashcards for durability.
3. To make extra flashcards, photocopy the flashcard template (page 6) on card stock and fill in the cards with needed equations. Cut out and laminate for durability.
4. For a key to addition and subtraction facts with answers 0–12, see page 49.

$6 + 4$

$6 - 1$

$7 + 3$

$12 - 6$

$8 + 2$

$11 - 5$

$9 + 1$

$10 - 4$

$1 + 10$

$9 - 3$

$2 + 9$

$8 - 2$

41

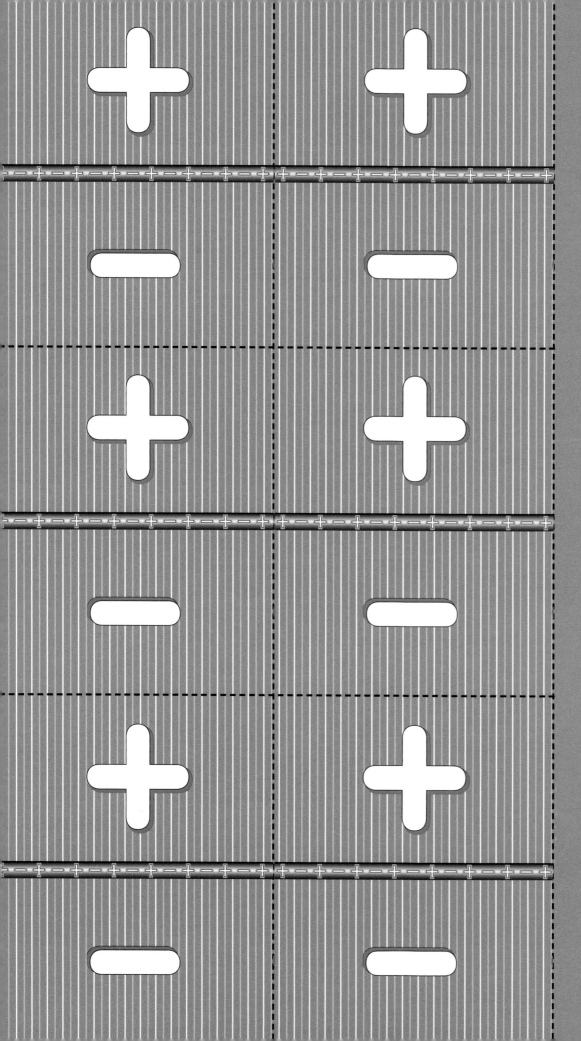

PUNCH-OUT ADDITION/SUBTRACTION FLASHCARDS

Here's how to create your set of 72 flashcards:

1. Punch out each flashcard by gently tearing around the perforated edge until the card comes loose.

2. Laminate flashcards for durability.

3. To make extra flashcards, photocopy the flashcard template (page 6) on card stock and fill in the cards with needed equations. Cut out and laminate for durability.

4. For a key to addition and subtraction facts with answers 0–12, see page 49.

43

3 + 8	4 + 7
7 − 1	12 − 5
5 + 6	6 + 5
11 − 4	10 − 3
7 + 4	8 + 3
9 − 2	8 − 1

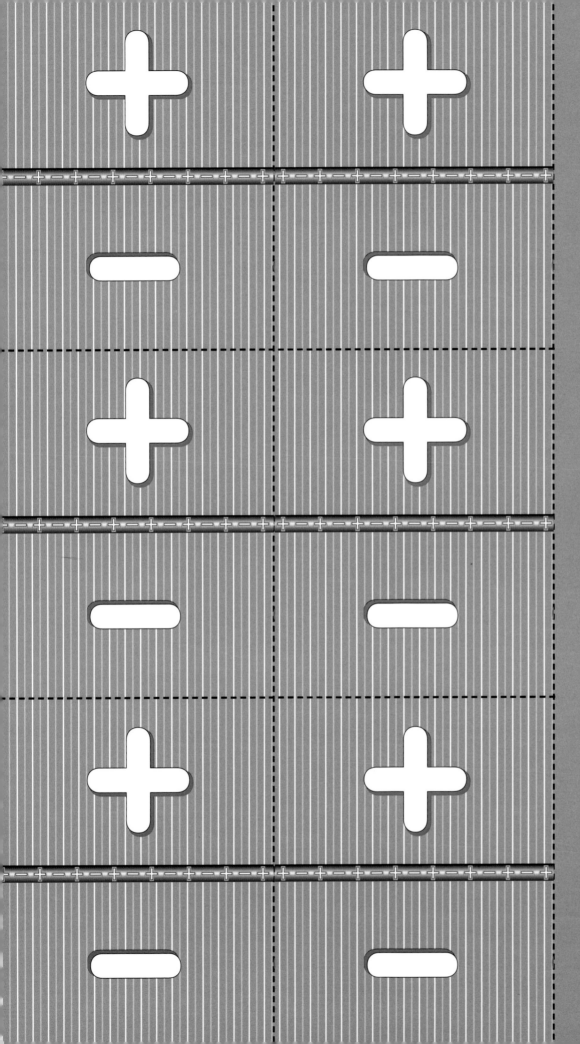

PUNCH-OUT ADDITION/SUBTRACTION FLASHCARDS

Here's how to create your set of 72 flashcards:

1. Punch out each flashcard by gently tearing around the perforated edge until the card comes loose.
2. Laminate flashcards for durability.
3. To make extra flashcards, photocopy the flashcard template (page 6) on card stock and fill in the cards with needed equations. Cut out and laminate for durability.
4. For a key to addition and subtraction facts with answers 0–12, see page 49.

$9 + 2$

$12 - 4$

$1 + 11$

$11 - 3$

$2 + 10$

$10 - 2$

$3 + 9$

$9 - 1$

$4 + 8$

$12 - 3$

$5 + 7$

$11 - 2$

45

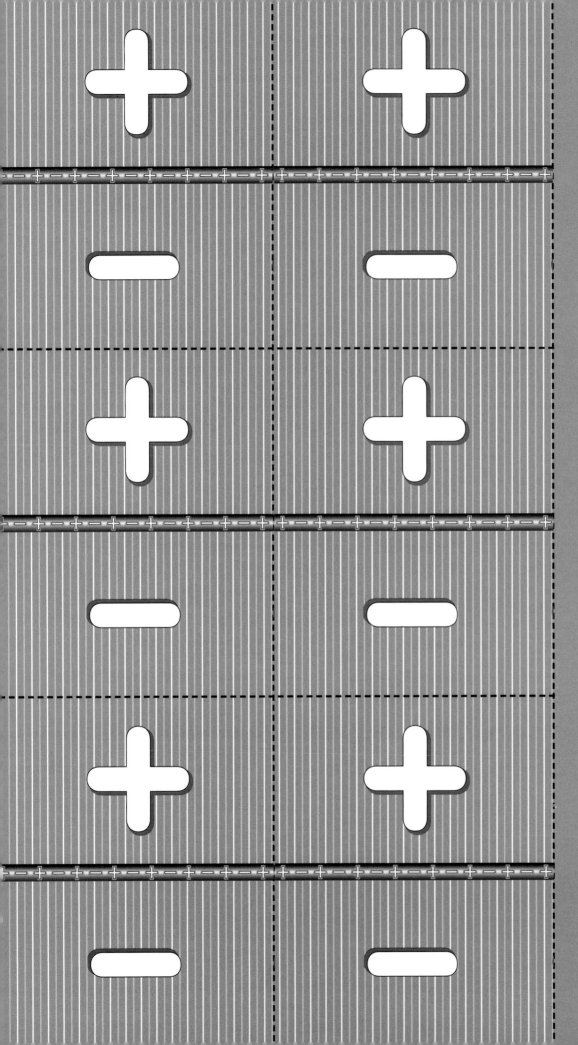

PUNCH-OUT ADDITION/SUBTRACTION FLASHCARDS

Here's how to create your set of 72 flashcards:

1. Punch out each flashcard by gently tearing around the perforated edge until the card comes loose.

2. Laminate flashcards for durability.

3. To make extra flashcards, photocopy the flashcard template (page 6) on card stock and fill in the cards with needed equations. Cut out and laminate for durability.

4. For a key to addition and subtraction facts with answers 0–12, see page 49.

$6 + 6$

$10 - 1$

$7 + 5$

$12 - 2$

$8 + 4$

$11 - 1$

$9 + 3$

$12 - 1$

$10 + 2$

$11 - 0$

$11 + 1$

$12 - 0$

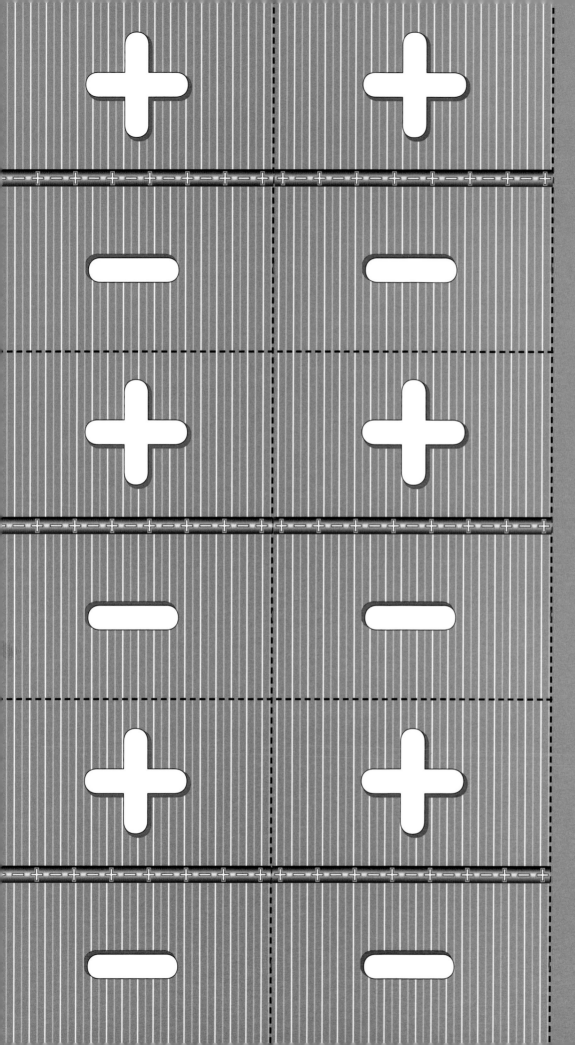